William Bolcom

T0087627

Old Addresses

for Baritone Voice and Piano

ISBN 978-1-4234-2703-2

EDWARD B. MARKS MUSIC COMPANY / **Exclusively Distributed By** HAL•LEONARD® CORPORATION

7777 W. BLUEMOUND RD. P.O. BOX 13819 MILWAUKEE, WI 53213

EDWARD B. MARKS MUSIC COMPANY AND BOLCOM MUSIC
126 East 38th Street
New York, New York 10016

www.ebmarks.com
www.halleonard.com

2

PROGRAM NOTE

When Stephen Salters won the Naumburg and I was requested to write a cycle for him, I decided to give him seven poets' work that, together, would create a panoramic "fan" of songs. All the fans' vanes had to fit together well; one of the most difficult challenges in this cycle was finding the right set of poetic weights and shapes to accomplish this. So many wonderful options were considered and rejected, and I was surprised at how hard it would be to select this set of poems. But I think this group fits together in some probably inexplicable way.

"Lady Death" brings back the direct verbal wallop I sometimes felt at North Beach poetry readings during my college days in the Bay Area (I imagine I might even have heard A.D. Winans reading at one, or on KPFA), but there's also something almost French in the *art-brut*, in-your-face inexorability of this poem. C.P. Cavafy, the great Cairene poet of a century ago (here translated by Rae Dalvan), contributes an elegant vignette from his homoerotic prowls, "The Next Table," full of the urbane, rueful humor so typical of him—unfortunately the very sort of thing that might land him in jail in today's Egypt. Ezra Pound's early "Histrion" (the Greek word for actor) wonders at the departed spirits of the great that seem to replace Pound's own within him, so deeply that his own soul seems sometimes effaced.

As with William Blake, one senses that so many of Langston Hughes' poems seem to have an implicit tune the poet might even have composed and thrown away; I find "Ballad of the Landlord" definitely in this vein. The Provincetown poet Mark Doty's "The Embrace" heartbreakingly chronicles a dream visit from a lover who has died. The Black Panther George Jackson's wonderful letters from Soledad Prison contain this ecstatic portrait, "Africa," here faithfully reworked by Arnold Weinstein into a lyric. With a very New York boulevard poem reminiscent of French surrealistic humor, Kenneth Koch's "To My Old Addresses" completes the set.

WILLIAM BOLCOM

Commissioned by The Walter W. Naumburg Foundation

World Premiere, Alice Tully Hall, April 29, 2002, by
Stephen Salter, Baritone, 1999 Naumburg Vocal Award,
and David Zobel, Piano

OLD ADDRESSES
A Song Cycle for Baritone and Piano

CONTENTS

Duration: *ca.* 24 minutes

GUIDE TO IDIOMATIC NOTATION

Three forms of notation indicate other than normal singing tone. These are indicated as follows:

In figure 1, normal noteheads with x's through their stems (which looks like Schoenbergian *Sprechstimme*) here indicate a general allusion to pitch, but in a speaking tone.

In figure 2, the x-noteheads give the general contour of the line, but pitches are not as important as in figure 1. The notes are spoken.

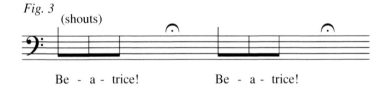

Stems without noteheads just give the rough shape of that spoken line.

ACCIDENTAL POLICY

Accidentals obtain throughout a beamed group. Unbeamed notes within a measure continue the same accidental until interrupted by another note or rest (the additional courtesy accidentals reduce the need to return the eye to the beginning of a measure). In music with key signatures, traditional rules apply.

for Stephen Salters and Shiela Kibbe

OLD ADDRESSES
Lady Death

A.D. WINANS

WILLIAM BOLCOM

*   for small hands, omit G, l.h.

sam - son's hair   she was the   last   ro - man sol - dier at the cru - ci -

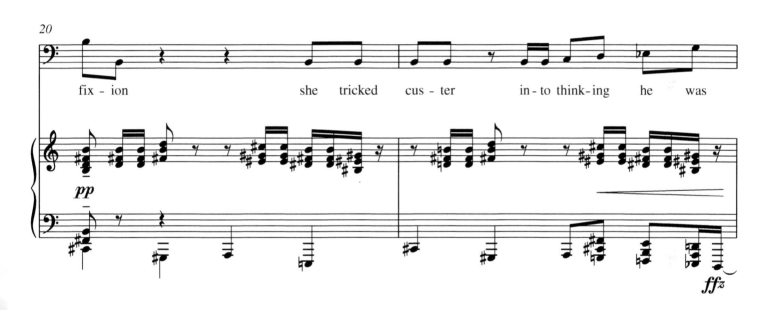

fix - ion   she tricked cus - ter   in - to think - ing he was

god   she's hard - er than a pimp   she's

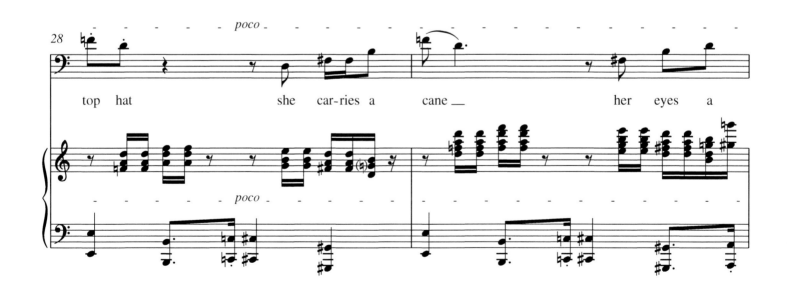

The Next Table

C.P. CAVAFY

WILLIAM BOLCOM

Languorous, ♩. **= 54 (in one),** *with bemusement*

He must be

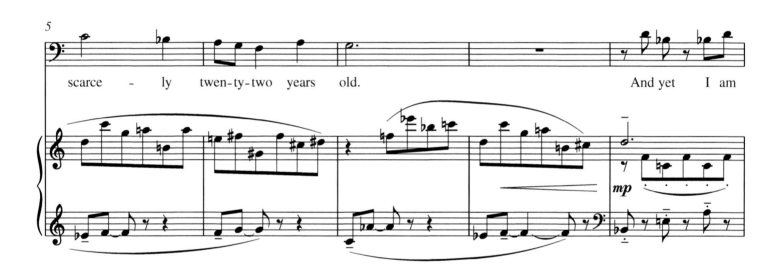

scarce - ly twen-ty-two years old. And yet I am

cer - tain that near-ly as man-y years a - go, I en - joyed the

know _____ eve - ry move - ment   he makes—   and be - neath   his clothes, _

once   more _____   I   see _____

_ the   be - lov - ed   bare   limbs. _____

Histrion

EZRA POUND

WILLIAM BOLCOM

Histrion

poco rit.　　　　a tempo

and are not Save re‑flex‑ions of their souls.

Thus am I Dan‑te for a space and am One Fran‑cois Vil‑

lon, bal‑lad‑lord and thief Or am such ho‑ly ones I

may not write Lest blas‑phe‑my be writ a‑gainst my name; This for an

in - stant   and the flame _____   is   gone _____   'Tis   as   in

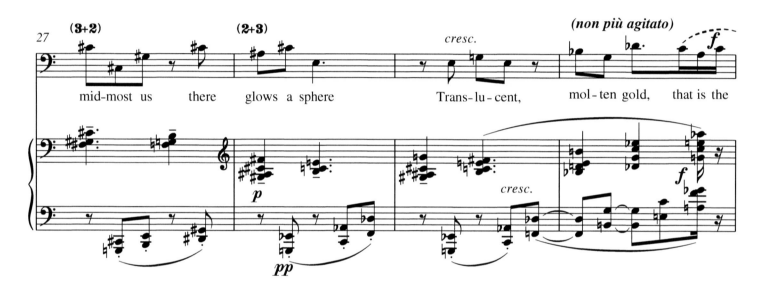

mid-most us   there   glows a sphere   Trans-lu - cent,   mol - ten gold,   that is the

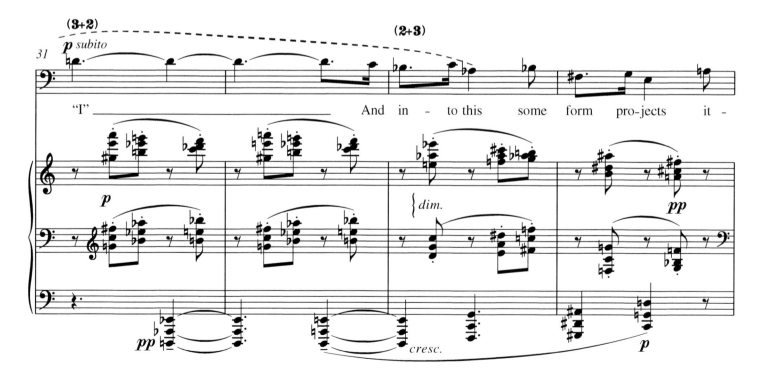

"I" _____   And   in - to this   some   form   pro - jects   it -

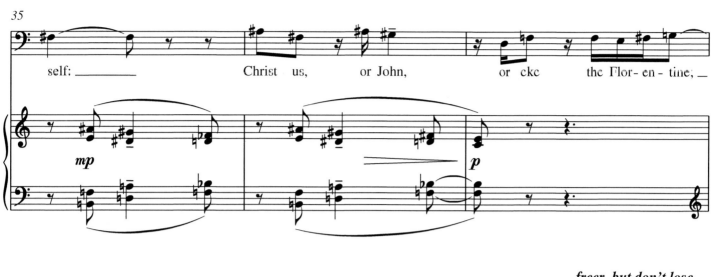

self: _____   Christ us,   or John,   or eke   the Flor- en - tine; _

freer, but don't lose rhythmic shape

And   as the clear

space is not   if a form's Im-posed there - on, _____   So ___ cease we _

Ballad of the Landlord

LANGSTON HUGHES

WILLIAM BOLCOM

you come up __ your - self __ it's a won-der you don't fall down.

Ten Bucks you say I owe you? Ten Bucks you say is due? Well, that's

Ten Bucks more - 'n I'll pay __ you Till you fix this house up new.

What? You gon-na get e-vic-tion or-ders? You gon-na cut off my heat?

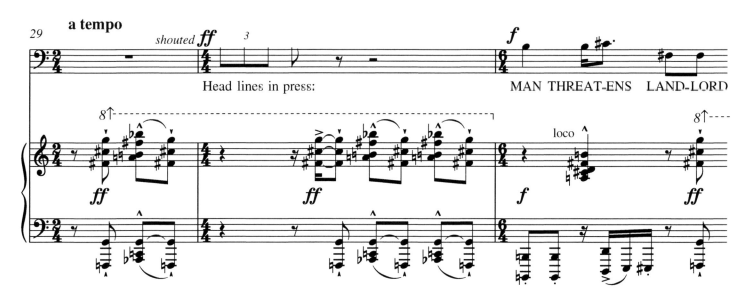

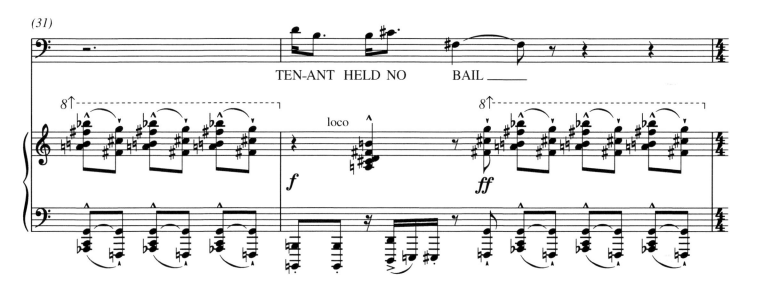

*Small hands need not play R.H. bottom notes

The Embrace

MARK DOTY

WILLIAM BOLCOM

Molto moderato ♩ = 60

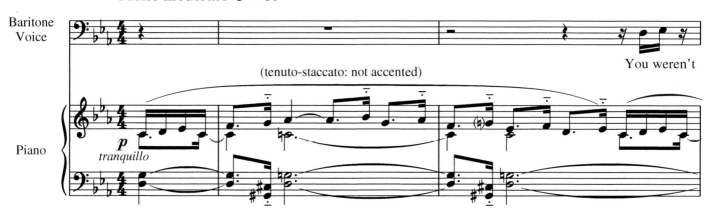

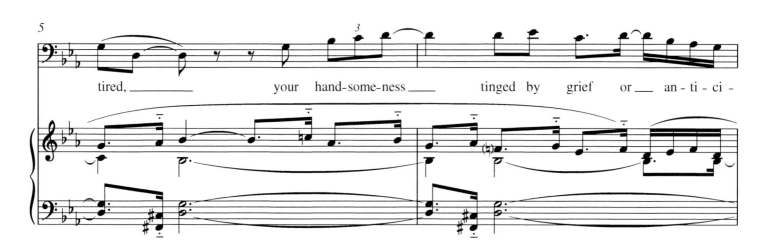

true still,   e - ven   in the dream. _____

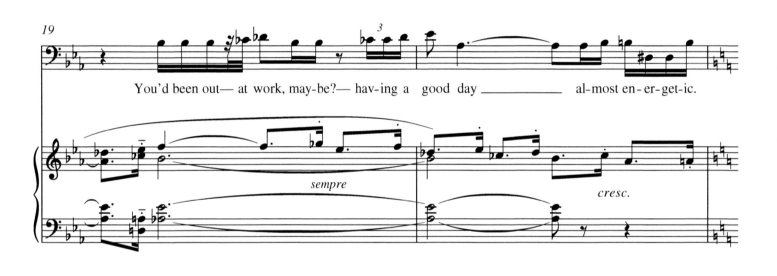

You'd been out— at work, may-be?— hav-ing a   good day _____ al-most en-er-get-ic.

sempre   *cresc.*

We   seemed   to   be   mov - ing   from   some

mf   *p*

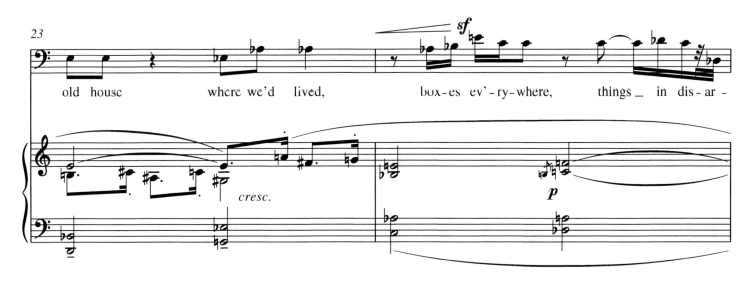

old house where we'd lived, box-es ev'-ry-where, things __ in dis - ar -

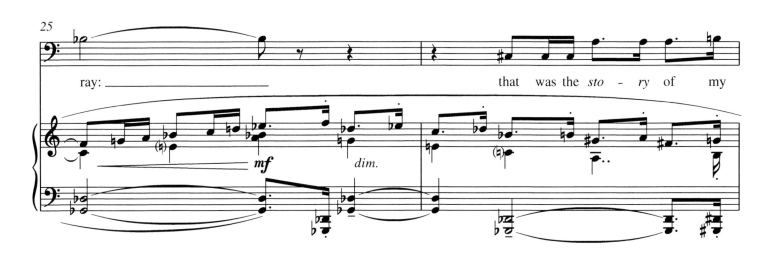

ray: ____ that was the *sto - ry* of my

dream _____ but e - ven a-sleep I was shocked out of

The Embrace

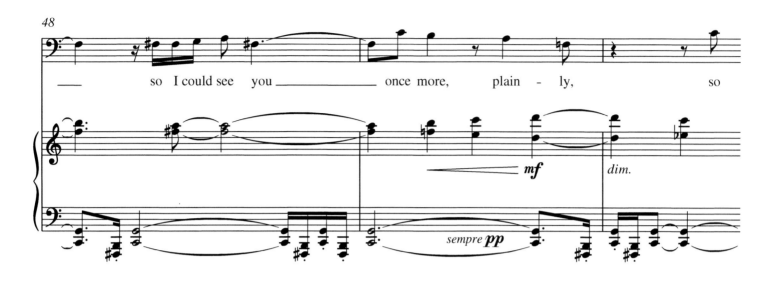

so I could see you _____ once more, plain - ly, so

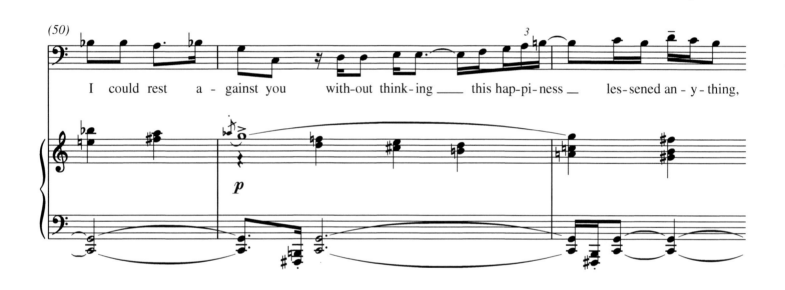

I could rest a - gainst you with-out think-ing ____ this hap-pi-ness ___ les-sened an - y - thing,

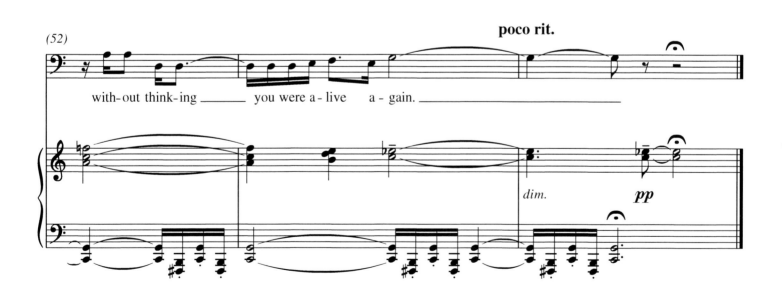

with-out think-ing _____ you were a - live a - gain. _____

Africa
(adapted from a prison letter of George Jackson)

ARNOLD WEINSTEIN

WILLIAM BOLCOM

mil - lion years a - go Were found _____ be - low the ground in Af - ri - ca __

__ The old - est cit - ies in ___ the world in Af - ri - ca. ____ The old - est

lan-guage in ___ the world_ in Af - ri - ca, Af - ri - ca, Af - ri - ca!

Eve - ry kind of peo - ple, eve - ry kind of shade, An - y col - or

long long while __ To tell of eve - ry peo - ple eve - ry style _____ The _

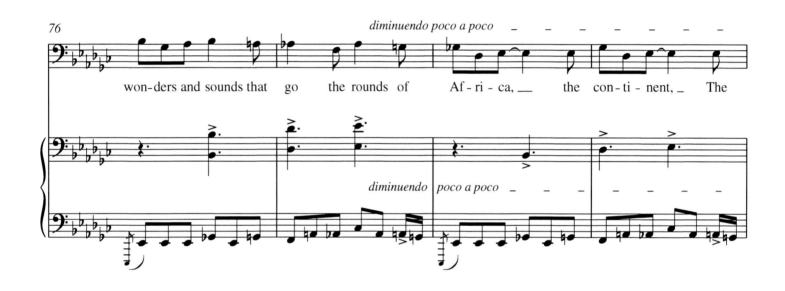

won-ders and sounds that go the rounds of Af - ri - ca, __ the con - ti - nent, _ The

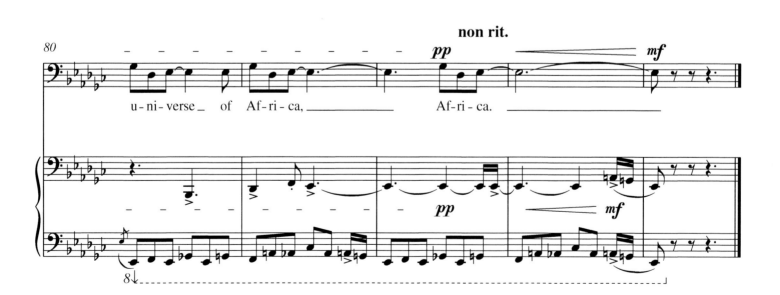

u - ni - verse _ of Af - ri - ca, _____ Af - ri - ca. _____

This page blank to facilitate upcoming page turns

To My Old Addresses

KENNETH KOCH

WILLIAM BOLCOM
(2001)

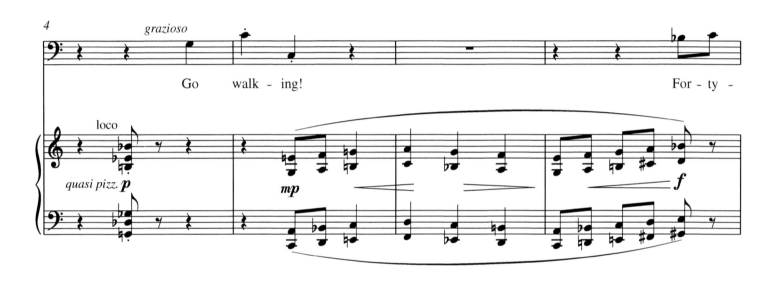

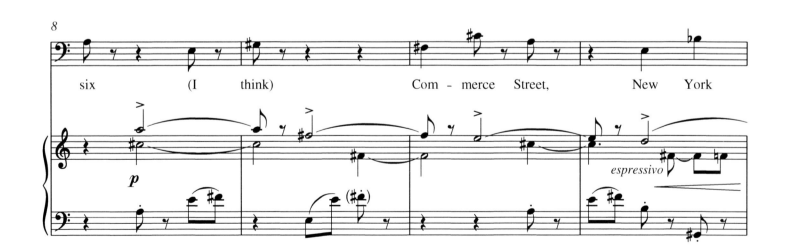

* French pronunciation: "Par-*ee*"

To My Old Addresses

Num-ber 2, in Clat-ter-y, Mich-i-gan George Wash - ing-ton Mod-el Air - plane School, Bis - bee, Ar - i - zo - - na Won-der-land, the stone

* German pronunciation: "*Vol*-pay"

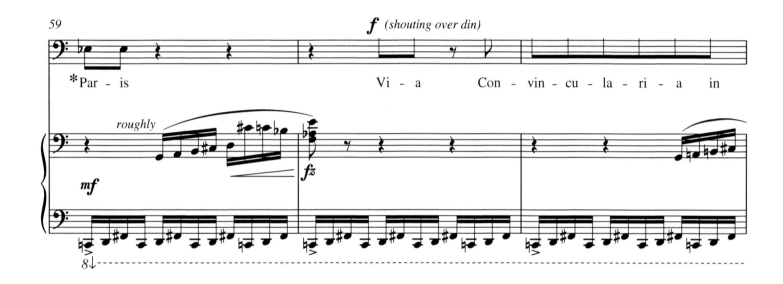

*English pronunciation

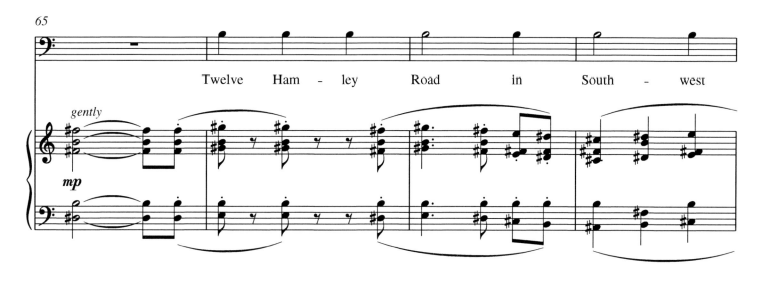

Twelve Ham - ley Road in South - west

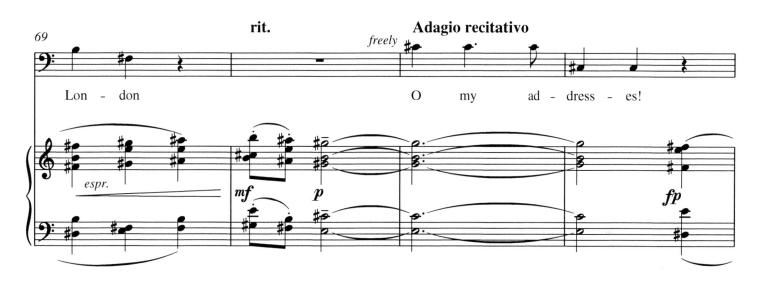

rit.   **Adagio recitativo**

Lon - don   O my ad - dress - es!

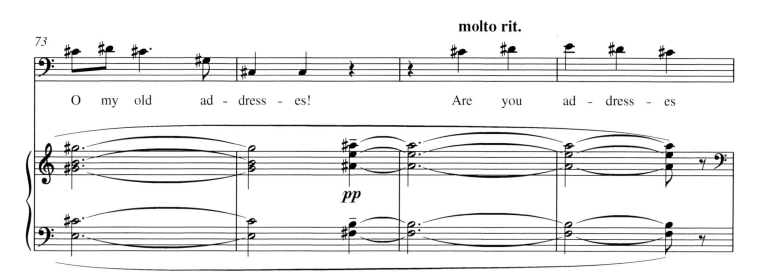

molto rit.

O my old ad - dress - es!   Are you ad - dress - es

most ly to know if you are well. I ____

___ am all right but I think I will nev - er find ___

___ Sus - te - nance as I found in you, oh old ad -

*small notes: *ossia*

I. Lady Death

she holds the trump card
in a fixed game
she brought the iron man
lou gehrig to his knees
mocked babe ruth
at home plate
she skulks around
the circus grounds
looking for an accident
to happen

she was the last person
at the Alamo
she fed lorca a meal
of bullets
she waited table
at the last supper
she hired the barber
who cut samson's hair
she was the last
roman soldier at the
crucifixion
she tricked custer
into thinking he was
god
she's harder than
a pimp
she's cunning
she's cruel
she's after me
she's after you
she wears a top hat
she carries a cane
her eyes a dagger
aimed at your heart

–A.D. Winans
© 1999 by A.D. Winans. Used by permission.

II. The Next Table

He must be scarcely twenty-two years old.
And yet I am certain that nearly as many
years ago, I enjoyed the very same body.

It isn't at all infatuation of love.
I entered the casino only a little while ago;
I didn't even have time to drink much.
I have enjoyed the same body.

If I can't recall where–one lapse of memory means nothing.

Ah see, now that he is sitting down at the next table
I know every movement he makes–and beneath his clothes,
once more I see the beloved bare limbs.

–C.P. Cavafy

III. Histrion

No man hath dared to write this thing as yet,
And yet I know, how that the souls of all men great
At times pass through us,
And we are melted into them, and are not
Save reflections of their souls.
Thus am I Dante for a space and am
One François Villon, ballad-lord and thief
Or am such holy ones I may not write,
Lest blasphemy be writ against my name;
This for an instant and the flame is gone.

'Tis as in midmost us there glows a sphere
Translucent, molten gold, that is the "I"
And into this some form projects itself:
Christus, or John, or eke the Florentine;
And as the clear space is not if a form's
Imposed thereon.
So cease we from all being for the time,
And these, the Masters of the Soul, live on.

–Ezra Pound

IV. Ballad of the Landlord

Landlord, landlord,
My roof has sprung a leak.
Don't you 'member I told you 'bout it
Way last week?

Landlord, landlord
These steps is broken down.
When you come up yourself
It's a wonder you don't fall down.

Ten bucks you say I owe you?
Ten bucks you say is due?
Well, that Ten Bucks more'n I'll pay you
Till you fix this house up new.

What? You gonna get eviction orders?
You gonna cut off my heat?
You gonna take my furniture and
Throw it in the street?

Um-huh! You talking high and mighty.
Talk on – till you get through.
You ain't gonna be able to say a word
If I land my fist on you.

Police! Police!
Come and get this man!
He's trying to ruin the government
And overturn the land!

Copper's whistle!
Patrol bell!
Arrest.

Precinct Station.
Iron cell.
Headlines in press:

48

MAN THREATENS LANDLORD

TENANT HELD NO BAIL

JUDGE GIVES NEGRO 90 DAYS IN COUNTY JAIL.

–Langston Hughes

V. The Embrace

You weren't well or really ill yet either;
just a little tired, your handsomeness
tinged by grief or anticipation, which brought
to your face a thoughtful, deepening grace.

I didn't for a moment doubt you were dead.
I knew that to be true still, even in the dream.
You'd been out – at work maybe? –
having a good day, almost energetic.

We seemed to be moving from some old house
where we'd lived, boxes everywhere, things
in disarray: that was the *story* of my dream
but even asleep I was shocked out of narrative

by your face, the physical fact of your face:
inches from mine, smooth-shaven, loving, alert.
Why so difficult, remembering the actual look
of you? Without a photograph, without strain?

So when I saw your unguarded, reliable face,
your unmistakable gaze opening all the warmth
and clarity of you – warm brown tea – we held
each other for the time the dream allowed.

Bless you. You came back, so I could see you
once more, plainly, so I could rest against you
without thinking this happiness lessened anything,
without thinking you were alive again.

–Mark Doty

VI. Africa
Adapted from a prison letter of George Jackson

Africa?
You ask me about Africa?

Let me relate the wonder
Of the place called Africa

There's every treasure on the earth
and in the earth of Africa
Iron in Liberia
Diamonds in Nigeria
Gold in Zambia
Though Europe mined it
Name it you'll find it
In Africa.

South of the Sahara
On down to the Cape
You find the finest lands
And natural hands to farm it.

Tanzania a giant jungle garden
The temperature is mild,
The whole year through
In Africa

The oldest remains
Of those who roamed the plains a million years ago
Were found below the ground
Of Africa
The oldest cities in the world in Africa
The oldest language in the world of Africa!

Every kind of people, every kind of shade
Any color too,
Lightest ivory to blackest blue!
Every shape every face:
wide nose, thin nose, aquiline,
Curls in thick rows,
Or hair delicate and fine.

Oh it would take me a long long while
To tell of every people every style
The wonders and sound
that go the rounds
Of Africa, the continent,
The universe of Africa.

–Arnold Weinstein

VII. To My Old Addresses

Help! Get out of here! Go walking!
Forty-six (I think) Commerce Street, New York City
The Quai des Brumes nine thousand four hundred
    twenty-six, Paris
Georgia Tech University Department of Analogues
Jesus Freak Avenue No. 2, in Clattery, Michigan
George Washington Model Airplane School,
    Bisbee, Arizona
Wonderland, the stone font, Grimm's Fairy Tales
Forty-eight Greenwich Avenue the landlady has a dog
She lets run loose in the courtyard seven
Charles Street which Stefan Wolpe sublet to me
Hotel de Fleurus in Paris, Via Convincularia in Rome
Where the motorcycles speed
Twelve Hamley Road in Southwest London O
My addresses! O my old addresses! Are you addresses still?
Or has the hand of Time roughed over you
And buffered and stuffed you with peels of lemons,
    limes, and shells
From old institutes? If I address you
It is mostly to know if you are well.
I am all right but I think I will never find
Sustenance as I found in you, oh old addresses
Numbers that sink into my soul
Forty-eight, nineteen, twenty-three, O worlds in which
    I was alive!

–Kenneth Koch